Mack Made Movies

DON BROWN

ROARING BROOK PRESS
Brookfield, Connecticut

Copyright © 2003 by Don Brown

Published by Roaring Brook Press

A division of The Millbrook Press, 2 Old New Milford Road, Brookfield, Connecticut 06804

Library of Congress Cataloging-in-Publication Data

Brown, Don.

Mack made movies / Don Brown.—1st ed.

p. cm.

Summary: A simple biography of the director whose silent films immortalized such slapstick clowns
as the Keystone Kops, Charlie Chaplin, Fatty Arbuckle, Mabel Normand, and Ben Turpin.

1. Sennett, Mack, 1880-1960—Juvenile literature. 2. Motion picture producers and directors—Canada—Biography—
Juvenile literature. 3. Motion picture actors and actresses—Canada—Biography—Juvenile literature. [1. Sennett, Mack,
1880-1960. 2. Motion picture producers and directors.] I. Title.

PN1998.3.S43 B76 2003   791.43'0233'092—dc21   2002006357

ISBN 0-7613-1538-1 (trade edition)   10   9   8   7   6   5   4   3   2   1
ISBN 0-7613-2504-2 (library binding)   10   9   8   7   6   5   4   3   2   1

Printed in the United States of America

First edition

For Kathy and Mack

In 1900, twenty-year-old Mack Sennett was a horse's rear end.

It was just a silly role in a foolish skit on a shabby Manhattan stage, but it was his stage debut and Mack dreamed of being a show business star.

Had his simple, hardy life made him ache for something different and glamorous? Young Mack had grown up on a Canadian farm. He had hammered rivets and ladled molten metal as an ironworker. Silly or not, a horse's rear end was a step toward his dream.

Besides, as the actor playing the front legs explained, "The hind legs do all the acting and get all the applause!"

In search of more applause, Mack acted, clowned, sang in quartets and trios. He carried scenery.

He tried out for a musical and was asked to show his dancing skills. After a few clumsy steps, the star of the show said, "Please remove this bumbler."

Audiences could be mean, too.

THEY NEVER APPLAUDED. THEY GAVE THE RAZZBERRY TO EVERY EFFORT.

Despite the disappointments, Mack didn't quit. He learned slapstick—a kick-in-the-pants, slip-on-a-banana-peel kind of physical humor. It was loony, acrobatic, and rough-and-tumble. In slapstick skits, things go wrong and events spin out of control, unraveling until all that's left is pandemonium.

Audiences loved it. Mack did, too.

He performed in lots of big cities, like New York, Chicago, and Boston. But the roles were small and success seemed far off.

Between jobs, Mack lived on five-cent lunches and rented rooms in cheap boardinghouses with other rag-tag show business hopefuls: "Midgets, fat ladies, tap dancers, carnival entrepreneurs, and unemployed snake charmers." His worried mother mailed him $20 bills.

But a man who was willing to play a horse's rear end doesn't give up easily. Mack decided to try the movies.

Movies were a new sensation. In 1892, famous inventor Thomas Edison introduced the Kinetoscope. For a nickel, the box-shaped device played a tiny film viewed through a peephole. Early films had no story or acting; the first movie just showed a man sneezing! Early films had no sound, and movies were silent for about thirty more years. Still, movies thrilled people. Movies seemed *alive*.

In 1896, films came out of the Kinetoscope and were projected onto screens. Movie theaters sprang up across the country. The theaters were called nickelodeons, because admission was a nickel and "odeon" is the Greek word for theater. By 1909, three million people a day were visiting nickelodeons.

EARLY CAMERAS WERE
HAND POWERED.

EARLY FILM RECORDED
IMAGES ONLY IN BLACK AND
WHITE. COLOR FILM WASN'T
COMMON UNTIL THE 1950'S.

THE CAMERA CAPTURES
THE ACTION AS A SERIES
OF STILL PICTURES.

THE STILL PICTURES
ARE DISPLAYED QUICKLY
ONE AFTER ANOTHER
TO GIVE THE IMPRESSION
OF MOVEMENT.

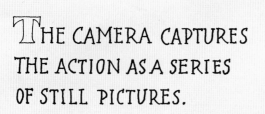

FLIP THE PAGES TO WATCH THE DOG DANCE

From the nickelodeons came a cry for movies, movies, movies! All sorts of unlikely people—"sweatshop operators, bicycle repairmen, or cloak-and-suit manufacturers"—rushed into the moviemaking business. The Warner brothers created one of the world's biggest film companies with the money they raised by selling their family's horse. Carl Laemmle stopped selling clothes to start making movies and became the boss of Universal Pictures.

On January 17, 1909—his twenty-ninth birthday—Mack landed a job with the Biograph movie company, and threw himself into the task of learning how to make films. He toted cameras, shifted scenery, acted, wrote, and directed.

Moviemaking proved to be as troublesome as dancing. The cameras were cranked by hand, and if they were cranked too slowly, the actors on film appeared to jump around like kangaroos. If cranked too fast, the picture seemed to crawl in slow motion. Early movies were lit with free sunshine and filmed outdoors. Rain and clouds stopped work.

Mack learned the moviemaking craft. Then he remembered his days on stage and had a tall idea: He thought that slapstick would be as popular with movie audiences as it was with theatergoers. Mack was certain he was right, but his bosses at Biograph were more interested in making romances and dramas.

I COULDN'T GET THE COMEDY IDEA OUT OF MY HEAD AND FINALLY PERSUADED TWO OTHER FELLOWS TO GO INTO PARTNERSHIP WITH ME ON PRODUCING COMEDIES.

He decided to follow other moviemakers to southern California. The sunshine and clear skies needed for moviemaking were abundant there. Mack built a studio, which he called Keystone Pictures, near the former lemon and orange groves known as Hollywood.

EVERY MORNING, I WENT TO THE STUDIO AND GOT PROPS READY FOR THE DAY'S WORK. I WAS TELEPHONE OPERATOR, BOOKKEEPER, ACTOR, DIRECTOR AND FILM CUTTER. IT TOOK A LOT OF PHYSICAL ENDURANCE TO GET THROUGH THE WORK. MY HAIR TURNED WHITE.

He made 140 movies his first year in California, silly movies of
high jinks and hee-haw, goofy, guffawing, golly-gee movies
where people . . .

plunged into vats of plaster,

spilled soup down their pants,

crashed through collapsing furniture,

and slid and slipped, flipped and flopped, crashed, crumbled,
careened, collapsed, and somersaulted across the screen.

It looked dangerous, but Mack and his performers were careful and bad injuries were rare.

Actors dangled from flagpoles,

spilled down stairwells,

floundered in floods,

and ran riot in helter-skelter chases: people chasing people, people chasing cars, people chasing dogs, dogs chasing people—anything, as long as it was funny.

Eventually a thousand workers joined Mack at Keystone. He called the studio a "fun factory," but the frantic moviemaking shop was more like a madhouse. How could Mack watch over the cameramen, carpenters, writers, prop and makeup people? How could he watch over the slapstick performers, who Mack described as "daft as rabbits in the moonlight"? He built an office atop a tower in the middle of the movie lot. It had plenty of windows . . . and a giant tub!

I COULD LIE BACK AND THINK. I COULD BATHE AND SOAP AND SPLASH AND SHOUT ANYTIME OF THE DAY, AND KEEP AN EYE ON MY OUTRAGEOUS EMPLOYEES.

Mack invented the Keystone Kops, a group of bumbling policemen who seemed to be on a never-ending chase aboard an overloaded police car. Mack loved to film the car in a wild spin and show the Kops being thrown from it like water from a shaking dog!

He filmed Mabel Normand delivering the first pie-in-the-face to Ben Turpin, launching a bit of comedy nonsense that is still used in TV and movies.

Mack hired Charlie Chaplin, a little-known English comic who had no experience performing in movies. Chaplin quickly became an expert and succeeded at making films that were both hilarious and heartbreaking. At Mack's studios, Chaplin created a character known as the Tramp. As the Tramp, Chaplin became the greatest film comedian of all time.

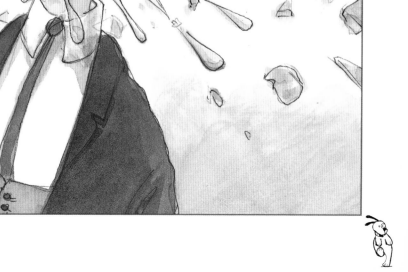

People said Mack's comedies were unlike anything else seen on screen. Mack's slapstick clowns—the Keystone Kops, Charlie Chaplin, Fatty Arbuckle, Mabel Normand, Ben Turpin, and many others—were more famous than presidents, prime ministers, and kings.

By 1916, 25 million people a day went to the movies, and Mack's funny, topsy-turvy, slapstick films which wobbled between the improbable and the impossible, were a favorite with audiences everywhere. Mack dubbed himself the King of Comedy, and nobody disagreed.

The horse's rear end *had* gotten all the applause.

Author's note

Mack Sennett was born in Richmond, Canada, on January 17, 1880. His family moved to Northampton, Massachusetts, when Mack was a teenager and he became a laborer at a New England ironworks. But for reasons even Mack couldn't adequately explain, he dreamed of a life as an opera singer. After consulting with a town lawyer, the future U.S. President Calvin Coolidge, Mack headed for New York City. But his dream was short-lived when he discovered that training for the opera would take years and offered no guarantee of success. Mack turned to burlesque, a style of low-brow entertainment that was wildly popular, and took work as a theater stagehand. When an actor failed to appear one night, Mack was drafted to replace him. From that accidental beginning Mack eventually made a modest theatrical career as a singer and comic. But he saw little hope for greater success and decided to gamble on the movies.

Nickelodeons seemed to be opening everywhere, and the demand for new movies to exhibit in them was enormous. New York City blossomed with moviemakers, due in part to its pool of performers but also to the city's proximity to Thomas Edison's New Jersey lab. Although Edison hadn't invented motion pictures, he had acquired patents to the technology, and movie cameras had to be rented from him. In 1909, Mack joined Biograph films and met director D. W. Griffith, who was pioneering techniques of motion picture storytelling. The following year, Mack began directing films and found a large and enthusiastic audience for his slapstick comedies. His success rivaled that of his mentor Griffith, but Biograph never embraced comedy. When an offer to be a partner in his own company arrived, Mack leaped at the opportunity.

He established Keystone Pictures in 1912 and moved to California, joining a stream of moviemakers who were attracted by southern California's fair weather and cheap land, crucial elements for building successful studios.

An added incentive was the hope of escaping Thomas Edison's heavy-handed enforcement of his patents.

Mack Sennett's comedies became world-famous on the strength of his superb sense of comic timing and great eye for talent. His breakneck pacing left audiences breathless, and he discovered stars such as Mabel Normand, Fatty Arbuckle, Ben Turpin, Gloria Swanson, W. C. Fields, and Carole Lombard. In 1914, Mack launched the film career of Charlie Chaplin, perhaps the greatest comedian of all time. And it was on a Sennett stage that the most enduring of all slapstick gags, a pie-in-the-face, was invented.

Mack bought out his partners in 1915, renaming the studio Mack Sennett Studios. But the early movie industry was risky and by 1935 the studio was bankrupt. Mack lived the rest of his life in retirement; he died in 1960.

Bibliography

Quotations attributed to Mack Sennett in this book are taken from his autobiography, *King of Comedy*. (Garden City: Doubleday, 1954)

Brownlow, Kevin. *Hollywood: The Pioneers.* New York: Alfred A. Knopf, 1979.

Kerr, Walter. *The Silent Clowns.* New York: Alfred A. Knopf, 1975.

Lahue, Kalton C. *World of Laughter.* Normon: University of Oklahoma Press, 1966.

Lahue, Kalton C. and Bewer, Terry. *Kops and Custards.* Norman: University of Oklahoma Press, 1968.

Pratt, George C. *Spellbound in the Darkness.* Greenwich: New York Graphic Society, 1966.

This Fabulous Century 1910–1920, Alexandra: Time-Life Books, 1969.